AF266602

Toxic Happiness

Viktoria D. Bednarczyk

Toxic Happiness
Viktoria D. Bednarczyk

Editor: Jackie Brown

Published by Star House Publishing

For any information regarding permission contact
info@starhousepublishing.com
www.starhousepublishing.com

ISBN 978-1-989535-26-4

Printed in the United States of America
First publication, 2020.

for all those struggling with their own inner demons;

I believe you.
I hear you.
I experience them too.

Table of Contents

More Than Just "Too Happy"

Many of us have a grand vision for ourselves; we may aspire to become a parent or to have a promising career. Some of us move further and partake in the Olympics, become successful entrepreneurs or possibly best-selling authors. I will, however, tell you about a girl whose vision for herself became so grand that she whole-heartedly believed she was part of the second coming. She was convinced she was the Virgin Mary and eventually found herself in a psych ward for her 18th birthday. A girl once known for her above average intelligence, athletic endeavors and kind soul, was now locked in a psych ward for a lengthy two months, a vicious cycle that never ended. And was told she has a mental disorder.

That girl is me. I have bipolar disorder.

According to the doctors, bipolar is defined as a mood disorder that has episodes of both mania as well as depression. Mania is just like a sugar craving that never goes away. I describe it as doing something in excessive amounts, and not being able to rest even once I satisfy it. For instance, I tend to obsess over exercising and needing social contact when I go through my episodes of mania. Picture this: I am someone who likes to maintain an average exercise routine of 3-4 times a week for an hour at a time. When I was going through mania, I would quickly obsess over working out 3+ times a day for prolonged periods, which was very unusual for me. Moreover, for someone who was conscious of how to have healthy relationships with others, I would quickly fixate over wanting to see, talk to and be with people non-stop when experiencing mania. Not only this, I experienced episodes of high energy, moments where I slept for only 3 hours a night for months, moments where I was unable to differentiate between reality and delusion, and more.

With bipolar, depression also exists – it is essentially the opposite of mania and would also come uninvited in waves. It is equally damaging. When I experience depression, I experience brain fog, lack emotion/am neutral, never want to socialize with those I loved, and the list goes on.

After re-remerging from the hospital my first time and entering the "real world," I was faced with a couple of daunting questions. Who was I? Was there something fundamentally wrong with me? Who was I beyond my disorder? Could I ever trust my own thoughts again? One may think the answers to these questions unveiled themselves soon after the diagnosis; unfortunately, this was not the case. Even seven years after the diagnosis, currently at the age of 25, with countless episodes of devastating psychosis interspersed with disabling depressions, these questions remain unanswered. Is my life just going to be a big blur of hospital stays? I hope not.

When dealing with the unpredictability of bipolar disorder, I began viewing the world in a different light. I began to challenge the old sayings and adages such as the more work you put in, the more work you get out or time heals everything, ideas that our society has accepted as truths. I found out shockingly that even though I put a lot of work into my life, I was not getting much results back. There was no emergence of graduation pictures, diplomas or notable job positions, but that did not necessarily mean I was not content. I also witnessed first-hand that time did not heal everything; some things simply stay broken. One day I could be perfectly fine and attend college classes; a week later, I could be in a psychiatric unit.

I have had to learn to adapt to the rhythms of my disorder and although I am not my disorder, it will always be a part of me. I have accepted that I have to go with the flow.

Although the disorder itself is challenging to navigate, the secrecy involved in a mental illness diagnosis, particularly in the first couple of years, can be even harder and devastating for the psyche. When someone experiences a heart attack or stroke, it is likely that friends and family will be notified promptly. This was unfortunately not the case for me and many others I have met. It is likely that the diagnosis will be kept secret (except for immediate family), forcing the individual to maneuver through some very challenging experiences on their own. For example, I personally did not share my diagnosis with my best friend until a year after my first episode. I'm not entirely sure what I was fearful of, but at the time, my encounters with psychosis seemed so bizarre and foreign. How exactly was I supposed to explain that I believed I was part of the second coming without downplaying the seriousness of the situation?

The secrecy extended beyond just close friends. I had to explain my annual fall disappearances amongst my sport and school circles with excuses like, "oh, I just wasn't feeling well" or "oh, my iron was just low" when in reality, I was being hospitalized for very serious manic psychoses.

When the time came and I did choose to reveal my diagnosis with a select few, it's almost like I said in a whisper.

. . . bipolar . . .

A very liberating whisper I may add.

Now let's go further: In this book, I'm going to take you inside my head by means of poems, diary entries, and recollections where you can experience my fire and what is formally known as mania. Do not judge my actions until you explore my thoughts and feelings; they will put things in perspective for you. Concepts that you may have considered to be "crazy" will suddenly become fathomable, tolerable, and acceptable.

The poems you will be reading in this book are recollections from the point of view of a manic brain – these are poems I wrote through my journey, before, during, and after hospital visitations - just to illustrate how real these unreal phenomena really seem.

Don't expect a list of symptoms, those you can search up online. Instead, expect an adventure.

This book is divided into seven sections:
Toxic Love
Mania
Depression
Stigma
The Kind of Love I Imagine,
Regaining Identity
Seven Years Later

If you are a sufferer of bipolar disorder yourself, perhaps it would be appropriate to start with the section most pertinent to your recovery at this moment in time. Otherwise, start from the beginning, reading each and every line with an open mind and an open heart.

Toxic Love

i dream up lottery numbers
in my sleep,
i told him nervously.

i had a phase like that too,
he countered.
-one dreamer finds another.

i think
what attracted
me to you the most was:

every time
i went a little crazy,
i saw a hint
of that chaos reflected in you.
-you always had that spark in your eyes.

he
had the gift
of bilocation,
the
ability
to be in
two places
at once.
-at least according to my deluded brain.

when i tried
to speak to you

it felt like
i was singing along
to a particularly
challenging
rap song:

all the right words
eluded me.

i am certain
i spoke words
that do not even
exist;

syllables formed
in all the wrong places.

i
fell
apart.
-i think you made sense of my nonsense.

my
tongue
blurted out
i love you,
betraying the feelings
my heart had so carefully coveted
for the last ten years.
-it took just three words

this is
not love,

it's an
addiction.

it just deserves
another prescription.
-it's time i made a call to the doctor.

instead of loving
i worshipped.
i mistook
you,
my equal,
for a
god.
-it's about time i stop bowing at your knees.

i

shook

at the

thought

of *you*

with

someone

else.

-jealousy.

he

hated

me

with the

same

intensity

i loved

him.

-manic love.

you
require
too much
attention,
he said.

and in that moment
the clouds darkened,
my eyes blurred,
and a storm
of the highest magnitude
swept through my insides.

my diaphragm inverted,
my lungs immediately collapsed,
and my heart stopped beating.
ice pellets spread in all directions,
piercing through every vital organ in my body.
my bones shattered separately
and then all at once.

time stopped.
"we" stopped.
-never tell a girl she requires too much attention, never.

he couldn't match her fire.
he steered far away from her hospital gown attire.
he promised friendship.
he turned out to be a liar.
he fled the scene when the situation was dire.
he flat out crushed all her desire.
he turned the most composed of girls into a crier.
-ten years of friendship meant nothing to him.

i knew not
if your
reason
for leaving
was *me*
or
my illness.

what is worse
i knew not
if you
could
distinguish
between the two
    -hidden motives.

for a long time after he left
she shuddered
at anything that resembled
his almond brown eyes.

she did not fear him,
he had never done anything to hurt her.

rather she feared the feelings
that came with him:

the butterflies,
guilt, rejection, tears
the delusions.

-every man that passed me by in the mall looked like him.

when
i met you
i did not lose myself.

being lost
implies permanency.

i simply
misplaced
myself,

meaning
there is a
great likelihood
i will be found once again.
-lost and found.

spiciness
is not one of the tongue's
primary tastes.

it is
in fact
pain signals
sent out by one's nervous system.

my ordeal
with you
was
very
very
spicy.

-it was ghost pepper level kind of pain.

i was ill.
i said things
i shouldn't have said.
i did things
i shouldn't have done.

that
does not
make me
your inferior.

-since when is the silent treatment an okay way of working things out?

in
the end
you were
just another person
to write about.
-just a name in my diary.

your
fragmented
put-downs
formed
the architecture
for my
wholesome
verse.

-i took advantage of the pain.

our friendship
was alluringly toxic.

like a bath bomb
that very much craved some water,
i longed for you.

every
encounter left me fizzing,
losing a piece of myself
in exchange
for your warmth.

not long after,
i did
not know
where i ended and you began;
you consumed me.

-toxic love was the only love i knew.

i
was a
raging
fire,

you
were
gasoline,

when all i needed
was a douse
of water.

-you were the catalyst.

my
words
are the
punches
that
my arms
would not
throw.

-you left me bruised and broken.

and
even during
my most expansive manias,
your words
reduced
me
to
tears.
-or rather waterworks.

you were like a
birthday
candle
in that your
presence in my life
needed to be extinguished,
for my dreams to start coming true.
-it took more than one blow.

i had been taken into the grip of a venus fly trap:
chewed on and spit out,
left disfigured
with little means to rebuild.

it stood 6'0,
had hulk-like quads
and washboard abs for a stem,
protruding biceps for petals,
and lustful lips that swallowed me whole.

i had been warned not to entertain
a relationship with such a beast.
-i thought opposites attract?

i bought you a christmas gift,
an apology for my wrong doings.

i knew you were an innovative mind,
exploding with ideas,
so i thought
i would gift
you a journal.

i never did see you that christmas though.
in fact, i never saw you again.
i messaged and called.
no response.

the irony of it is that i now use that journal
to scribble down lines
of any residual thoughts i have of you.
it is full of sentiments that i could not quite
spit out in person.

it is anger, love, and resentment all in one
it is the goodbye i never got.
it is
my closure.

-bye.

i think back
to the last time i broke boards
and I scold myself for using wooden boards.
for just as my foot
broke the wood in half,
my illness broke us irreparably.

and i think of why
i had not used plastic boards,
the ones that could easily be
snapped back together
and i wonder if that would have
made a difference.

i think of all these things
and of how when i first got back from the hospital
your first words to me were:
how is the world, champ?
and how good that made me feel.

mostly i just wanted to say
I am sorry we could not stay friends.
-i'll remember to use plastic boards next time.

you offered to
edit my writing.
i bet you didn't know
you were the protagonist
of every love poem you
were about
to read.

-or perhaps antagonist.

Mania

my senses
are heightened.
they can be compared to that of a sergeant.

the sound of a car in the distance,
the chattering
of each individual leaf,
a squirrel hidden
behind some shrubs,
all register in my brain
with great accuracy.

music seems to acquire an entity of its own;
my brain detecting each word in the lyrics separately,
each instrument indivually.

the notes reveal a mysterious energy;
each note corresponding
to a series of well-choreographed dance moves
in my head.
-the magical side of mania.

and every december
i anxiously awaited my manic days,
prepared to be illuminated,
like a glow stick ready
to be snapped
in half,
with only two truths
to keep me company along the way:

1. this light was fake, it bore no resemblance to the warmth and authenticity of the sun.
2. this light would slowly expire, dying a slow death until it disappeared to nothingness.

-don't confuse mania with true happiness.

october, 2012

dear God,
i am going to change the world this coming 18th birthday.
i am going to show people how to love!
train beyond possibility!
help fight this egotistical world!
there is something deeper than the outside world
and I know it now but i must admit i am confused.
-grandiose thinking, the first sign of trouble.

october, 2012

dear God,
i do not know what is going on.
should I text him?
please, it would be so much easier
if he texted me first.
why me?
what are you doing?
i would do it, but i just do not know if i am crazy
or if this is what you really want.
stop the pain for the next ten minutes completely
and i will do it.
-grandiose thinking pt.2, the second coming.

october, 2012

dear God,
i will help you change the world
but tell whatever is giving me
this cold air to stop.
i need to go to anatomy tomorrow!
please let me live!
i am still human and i am only seventeen.
i need to stay sane and sleep.
-grandiose thinking pt. 3, accepting the mission.

i think for all of us
diagnosed there is a
before and after.

for some it is marked by a specific date.
for me it is 01/11/2012,
the day i ended up in emerg.
the day i got sick.
-the night of halloween, the morning of all saint's day.

you thought
you were the virgin mary, too?
imagine if both of you were in the same psych ward.
that would be funny.
-finding out others have experienced your kind of madness.

i sat in a waiting room.
it reminded me a lot of a jail:
four walls with a small slit as a window,
security at the door.
the room was empty
except for a hospital bed
and a white sheet.

i wore it around my head,
the same way mary would have worn it
2012 years earlier.
the kicking in my stomach
grew stronger.
maybe my
baby
would
make it . . .

-entering emerg, the immaculate conception.

i was in a
different room now.
a man in a uniform stood outside.
paladin security it read.

he handed me an egg sandwich
and urged me to eat.
i was not hungry.

he then
gestured to the clock and urged me to sleep.
it was two in the morning.
i was not tired.
-the friendly security guard.

med student –
“ do you know why you’re here?”

me-
“do i have schizophrenia?”

med student –
“no, ***bipolar*** we think.”
-the diagnosis.

i was handcuffed.
i was locked overnight.
i was stripped of my clothing.
i was pinned to the ground
with needles aimed at me.
my food was rationed.
my phone calls listened to.
my every move was on camera.
my showers could only be of a set temperature.
i felt
like a prisoner.
this felt like a jail.
-first thoughts of the psych ward.

being stripped of
your clothes
was like
being
stripped
of
your
identity.

-they need to make more fashionable hospital gowns.

we're
going to do
a three-point attachment,
the security guards explained.

essentially
they
attached
me
to
three points
on the
bed.

-the consequence for performing a stepping side kick
on the room window.

i discovered
channel 29,
much music,
which would be my mode of survival
for the next couple of months.

every day at 6 am,
i would slip into the
common room
and dance my heart out.

i did not really care
if anyone was in the room with me,
in fact, if they were,
i would put in an extra effort,
a performance in a way.

each song gave me a
subliminal message:
diamonds by rihanna,
try by pink,
wicked games by the weekend.

i was the girl who
never stopped dancing.

-everyone always knew who had the tv remote: me, of course.

more than half of the people
on the unit tonight
were under
the age
of 25.

it must be a full moon,
we concluded.
-mental illness hits young.

with my vivacious monologues
and passionate harmonies,
i put hollywood's
best to shame.

my wardrobe
department,
however,
was lacking.

the wrinkled hospital gown was not
bringing out my good side.
-i made the nurses' jobs more interesting.

eventually they
started letting me
wear my own clothes again.
i made sure to wear shirts and sweaters
that had my last name clearly printed along the back.

i wanted
my name to
be remembered.
i wanted
to be remembered as
the girl
who never
stopped fighting.
-i felt a little bit more like myself again.

it was not "the asylum" that i had seen portrayed
so many times in horror movies.
it was not quite how i
envisioned a
psych ward
to be.

it was a community
that valued the we over the i,
where individual differences were celebrated.

it was a community with a firm belief
in the goodness of strangers,
where if one person
was going through
a breakup,
the whole
unit was.

it was a community of people
who would sing you happy birthday
with such conviction,
you would swear they had known you your entire life.

there was a rhythm to it all:
the check-ins and the discharges,
the way one knew it was a saturday or sunday
because of an eerie type of silence
that migrated through the unit.
there was the palpable joy in the room
when the food lady rolled in with the food cart,
the comings and goings of well-intentioned visitors,
all of it
made things more bearable.

-it was a place that kept us safe and that is what is most important.

i held his hand tightly and said
they are coming.

who?
he asked.

my school,
they are going to save us.

i was sure of it.
what was taking them so long
i did not know,
but nobody came;
we were on our own.

before he left,
he whispered something in my ear:
i hear that they have cameras in the washroom
and then he was gone.
-patient 1, freedom.

he
looked
at me
with
wide
eyes
and said
poor joseph.
    -patient 2, feeding my delusions.

news of my delusional beliefs surrounding being pregnant
with God's child traveled fast amongst the patients:
so, did your water break?
a man said to me.

the whole room erupted
with laughter.
-i was not enjoying his comedic gestures, patient 3.

a woman held
both of my arms
and said
make a wish,
make a wish quickly
because they are watching me.
why was she being so nice to me
and who was she?

-was she a genie here to grant me my wish? patient 4.

so i have been studying the
exact angles of these cameras.
see the one over there?
if you position yourself here and
take one step to the left and then one step to the right . . .

here?

yes, right here.
now you should be completely
out of sight of all the cameras.
now (nudging me jokingly) it looks
like you are talking to yourself.
now they might think you really are crazy.

-these angles still do not capture my good side, patient 5.

i listened
with intrigue
to a boy whose daily 6 am routine
entailed sitting cross-legged and chanting
at the top of his lungs.

we sat in a broken
hospital bed
that had been pulled out into the hallway.
all the nurses were out of sight.

and then in one swift movement
he kissed me
on the neck.
never did i
imagine
that it would be
on a broken hospital bed,
in a psych intensive care unit,
that i would experience my first kiss.
-i did not see that one coming, patient 6.

i developed the mentality of terry fox.
i was going to run until i could not run anymore
and i was going to leave a trace
behind me just in case
my parents went out looking.

i did not settle for just a regular jog.
one house along the way
had a nice-looking swing on it
attached to a tree.
so i went ahead and took a few swings,
all in good spirit.

15 min in i realized that i had not
put on any gloves.
i turned to the nearest house
and rang the doorbell.
a man who looked to be in his 30's came out.
i desperately asked him if he had any gloves to spare.
he came back with gardening gloves (yes, gardening gloves).
did they keep me warm?
no, but what was i expecting?
i had just walked up to a complete stranger's house
and asked for a pair of gloves.

-may i add it was –20 degrees out and i was jogging around in capris?

have
you ever
tried doing
pullups on the
subway?

no, but go
right ahead.

and that was enough
to set me off.
-subway adventures pt. 1.

i strutted up and down
the subway floor,
hanging on to the railing,
making sure that every step was in sync
with the beat of my music.
i started to pick up my pace to a little bit of a jog.

i spotted a woman carrying a timbit box from a distance.
there were still quite a lot of stations left until mine
and i was feeling hungry.

could I have one?
i asked in the nicest way possible.
she was hesitant but opened the box to offer me one.
-subway adventures pt. 2.

i climbed on top of the snowed-in school bus
parked in the school parking lot.
i began feeling this need
to "be risky."

the front of the bus had beams
crossing over one another.

i was tempted to see if
perhaps i focused
hard enough,
i could
balance on them.

i balanced on those beams with ease
and once i was done,
i proceeded to jump off the bus in the most graceful way possible,
brushing the snow off my shirt as i landed.
-superhuman me.

i twirled round and round,
carefully positioning my feet on the
highlighted pathway at the walt disney store.

the store was bustling with kids.
i watched as they picked out their latest elsa outfits.
zigzagging between the elsas,
there was the odd superman and batman.

i approached the designated movie watching area,
instantly mesmerized at how well
the children knew the let it go song.

i was their hero
i was their ice princess
but singing was not enough to prove who i was
the mini jetés,
which i executed flawlessly, i might add
sold the deal.

-elsa.

to identify with my experience,
it is not sufficient to take a broom between your legs
and imitate the likeness of lily potter.
you must understand that in my
moments of psychosis,
i did not merely pretend
to be lily potter,
i was lily potter,
wife of james potter,
mother of harry potter,
my senses convinced me so.
-i got lost in the world of my favorite childhood series.

i sat at the table,
pulling out my
carefully counted change.
i handed the waitress exactly six toonies and one loonie.
dinner was on me today.

i snapped a picture of my tea for insta
and started heading out.

as per vampire dietary guidelines,
my boyfriend did not
need to eat.
he was also invisible
(yet detectable through cold air gusts).

regardless, it was the perfect date.
i was the luckiest girl in the world.
might i add that all the tvs were
broadcasting for me,
as per his request.

-the vampire boyfriend.

my thoughts somehow led me to a flashback
from a movie i had seen long ago:
freaky friday.
if i dumped my head in the toilet
and held my breath
for long enough,
i would
switch
entities
with my twin.

so i did:
one
two
thr…….
oh, there you are.
a nurse conveniently showed up
through the bathroom door
with a slightly concerned look on her face.
she ruined my concentration.

-the things mania will get you to do.

she was
walking up the stairs.
suddenly the halo
over her head
vanished.
her entire body transformed into the grim reaper.
i had to face death head on,
with the axe and
everything

-formally known as an illusion.

rolled
off my bed.

instead of the
ground,
i was met with a cold cushion of air.

for the split-est of seconds,
i was floating,
hovering quite literally.

someone from the other side
decided to spare me of a disastrous fall.

instead, i descended to the floor
in a hot air-balloon-like fashion.
-mysterious air gusts.

for every apocalyptic tweet i sent out,
i heard a song in response.
these songs were not coming out of my phone
and only i could hear them.
there were many,
but only a few remain in my mind:
lady gaga's romance
africa
and then of course
the drums…

cold air
surrounded me.

i had a vision.
-auditory hallucinations.

i took a couple of my brother's possessions,
most notably his
army helmet
and hid it
in my closet.

i was fixed on the idea that if
i gathered enough items in my closet,
the positive energy would unveil a portal to a mystical world:
narnia (the one lily had uncovered in the chronicles of narnia).
-not many people get to meet aslan.

ever since my 18th,
my birthday's
been more
of a curse
than a blessing.

this year i celebrated with friends.
this year the curse ends.
-i spent my 18th, 19th and 20th birthdays in the psych ward.

it is christmas day.
we are having dinner at a family friend's house.
the top conversations for me to embarrass
myself with over dinner are:

1) time travel does not only exist,
   i have personally experienced it myself
   and would be delighted to share my experiences
   with everyone at the table.

2) harry potter is no longer merely a fictional story
   written by j.k. rowling.
   it is a real-life story that i
   have been chosen to be a part of.
   voldemort exists.

3) inception, also, in short, a real story.

-manic during the holidays pt. 2.

everyone was gathered in the common room.
a pizza pizza box lay unfolded
in the center.
i walked in through
the doorway to learn that
instead of our regular 11 pm curfew,
we were allowed to stay up until midnight
(which was a big deal).

the couches were occupied by patients
who watched the tv in awe,
as the miami heat
and raptors faced off.

the ball zoomed
from one player's hands to another at lightning speeds.
a streak of white followed each
and every single player.

they moved with such ease,
i could have sworn the entire match
was being planned telepathically.
i decided that if i focused well enough,
my positive energy could pierce through the tv screen
and influence the game.

i clenched my fists
and directed my attention to the screen.
-new year's eve, manic during the holidays.

date unknown

i felt that cold air again,
just as i did on halloween night.
i cannot believe this is really happening to me.
am i pregnant?
could i be?
five months?
i'm scared!

-the fourth "second coming."

i walked into the dojang.
they were making selections
for worlds.

he asked me if i was participating.
of course not.
did he not know i was pregnant (with God's child)?

pregnant people are not allowed
to be moving too much,
especially not participating in combat sports.
-in all other capacities, i could have easily competed that day.

april 23, 2015 @viktoriad991
10:36 am
you are lucky you are invisible
to the human eye.
the things you can get away with.

3:48 pm
how did you manage
to get into that bathroom, batman?
i thought it was secured.
must have watched prison break.
-a manic's twitter feed.

√ i need to take olanzapine.

√ i am not being controlled by ghosts.

√ i cannot talk to ghosts.

-a manic's checklist.

it starts with a song,
a love song,
because that's what
seems to be on the radio these days,
but then everything goes wrong.

all of a sudden, you are in love.
it no longer is just a song,
it is your song.

a couple days later you determine
it was written just for you,
you and him.

then you think the radio is
broadcasting just for you.
then it all starts spinning,
your world that is.
-how delusion creeps in.

when i am *manic*,
i am in a *gaseous* state.
my particles move
in a very disorganized fashion.
they crash into each other
and buzz out of sync.
i am explosive.
i am a vapor,
rising higher and higher into the sky.
i am on cloud 9.
my thoughts move so fast,
they diffuse into the air.

when i am *stable*,
i am in a *solid* state.
my particles form neat rows,
pressed close together,
side by side.
i am resilient.
i am not easily shaken.
i am able to withstand outside forces
that come my way.
my thoughts have substance.
i do not fear being broken.
i am the strongest in this state.

when i am *depressed*,
i am in a *liquid* state.
my particles are spread just enough,
that they can be easily manipulated.
i am vulnerable.
i take the shape of my container,
meaning i am willing to change myself
to please others.
i am the tears
that escape you after being broken up with.
i am the rain
that ruins your wedding day.
i am the water
that you wash your filthy hands in.
my thoughts are a flood of negativity.
i am at my worst in this state.
-the three states.

my writing mimicked
the patterns of my turbulent moods.
mania was a lot of scattered exclamation marks
and at times articulate sentences,
that constituted a lengthy portion of my diary.
its handwriting was hurried,
meandering between lines
and often illegible.

mania was interspersed
with vulgar language.
its themes were grandiose and always changing.
mania craved limericks and rhymes.
mania was innately creative.

depression was a lot of short sentences,
that almost never filled even a quarter of the page.
one could recognize the effort
with which i handwrote every single word.

depression was a lot of contractions:
many can'ts, don'ts, won'ts.
depression's main theme was failure and hopelessness.
its sentences were proper.
depression did not know rhyme.

-writing is healing no matter what the episode.

Depression

it was not just sadness,
it was leaving my bedroom
window wide open at night,
hoping someone would
kidnap me
while I slept.
- no one came.

i do not know who i am,
what i am.
i am in a distant world of my own.
people surround me
but i am numb.
-what kind of life is one where you cannot feel anything?

do you know how many more days
you have left of just waking up,
doing things, and going back to sleep?
17,000 days.

no, but i do not think about life that way.
-a conversation between a depressed versus non-depressed individual.

i was a playground in its winter months:
isolated, silent, abandoned
my swings creaked.
my slide was coated with ice.
my monkey bars gave out blisters
to anyone who dared approach my grounds.
my teeter-totter stood collapsed over to one side,
almost as if it preferred idleness over livelihood.
my sand did not get a glimpse of the sun.
i was smothered by the weight of the snow on my being.
i was defective.

-i felt like a nobody.

;
the decision to continue your life
rather than end it.
-semicolon.

in those moments you struggle to feel,
look to your body's instruments
to bring your emotions to life.
press your finger alongside the tears that escape your eyes.
look to them for sadness.
witness the corners of your mouth fold up into a smile.
look to it for joy.
use your fists to throw a couple punches.
look to them for anger.
and finally note the way your skin warms
when in close proximity to an admirer.
look to it for love.
-fake it until you make it.

a jigsaw piece,
cut out incorrectly,
i had straight edges all around.
my friends tried to
connect with me
but i was not
equipped
to do so.

-no one could reach me.

take an elastic band
and place it on your night table.

use it as a slingshot
anytime the monsters underneath your bed
decide to come for a visit.
-keep those monsters under control.

my soul is gone.
my soul is gone.
my soul is gone.
what the hell is wrong with me?
what the hell is wrong with me?
what the hell is wrong with me?
i just want to feel alive, that is all.
i just want to feel alive, that is all.
i just want to feel alive, that is all.
help me! help me! help me!
-repetition

i always aim to deliver the most authentic portrayal of my experiences for my readers. in regard to depression, i have considered simply leaving a couple pages completely blank with no writing at all. that was the true likeness of depression. it was nothing: no thoughts, no feelings, no social interaction, no writing. it was a complete nonexistence and i fear that no words can quite re-enact those feelings of emptiness.

-blank pages

Stigma

i

am

not a

monster.

-i am human, just like you.

tell me once more
that my delusions
are unreal,
my behavior inappropriate.
i dare you.
it sounds as ridiculous
as telling me there are
flamingos residing in antarctica.
-madness is hard to understand.

to answer your thoughts,
the pouch of fat on my front side is
no beer belly,
no freshman fifteen,
no baby bump,
no post breakup weight gain,
it is a medication belly:
a 30 lb gift from the pills i take that accompanies
every episode i have
-as if losing my mind is not enough torture already.

i think we all are a little bipolar,
she said.

i was fuming.
i wondered if my hair,
which had just been blow dried straight,
would suddenly burst into curls
from all the rage radiating
inside of me.
-a trip to the hair salon.

toronto has the cn tower.
new york has the empire state building.
france has the eiffel tower.
i am a city with buildings of my own:
athlete,
daughter,
sister.

in 2012 i had a major addition.
this building was of a sleek design.
it twisted and turned
forming unique angles.
it had a promising pool
and an elegant lobby.

this building surpassed the rest by metres.
it was called **bipolar**.
my biggest fear is that people will forget
about my other buildings,
that all they will see is bipolar.
-i am more than a disorder.

do not worry,
i have read all about
your illness!
a lot of famous people have it:
artists, singers, poets.
maybe you will be famous one day!
-misguided encouragement.

i gazed at my reflection in the mirror.
i took note of the tremor in my hands,
evidence of the lithium flowing through my veins.
i carefully examined my eyes
and wondered
if they revealed the heaviness inside me.
i looked at the extra twenty pounds on my frame,
swallowing a 0.5 mg lorazepam tablet as i did.
it was my version of a pre-date shot.
finally, i took a deep breath and reminded myself
this was a date, not a job interview.
-dating is stressful enough without mental illness.

i did not know how to *handle* it.
i think i might be able to *handle* it.
i do not think i could *handle* it.

three different guys.
one word in common.
"handle."

nothing about me needs to be handled.

-i am a woman of great complexities that deserves more than just to be handled.

when i was medicated,
i spoke,
i did not yell.
i was
rain, but not a flood.
wind, but not a hurricane.
heat, but not the sahara desert.
cold, but not polar ice.
light, but not a wildfire.
i felt comfortable with myself
and most importantly
i was a friend,
not a reckless,
irresponsible,
obsessive
coward.

-the good side to medication.

the meds,
they will numb you a little,
there is no doubt.
i felt as if i had been taking my tea
with two sugars my whole life
and then suddenly forced to
go down to none.

-everything around me just seemed a little less flavorful,
the bad side of meds.

in a manic frenzy, i once walked into a busy sports bar
and started doing pirouettes in the middle of the room.
i quickly learned that it was acceptable
to belittle those who are “crazy”.
the bar staff found it justified, for reasons
beyond my imagination, to charge me for my meal in advance.
-our culture panics when it has to deal with mental illness.

why do
your
hands
shake
like
that?
-a child's honesty.

i sought understanding.
i found it in poetry.
a poet's words brought my
experiences to life.
the dsm-5
did not.

-a newfound appreciation for art;
-dsm-5 is the diagnostic and statistical manual of mental disorders
-the handbook used by health care professionals to diagnose mental health disorders.

you are lucky
you have visitors,
she said.

no one comes to visit me.

-mental health patients deserve just as many get well soon cards as any other patients in the hospital.

too happy
does not do
my experience justice:
grandiose,
terrifying, humiliating
spiritual, psychotic, destructive,
yes.
but not
too happy.

-two words are not enough to describe the experience:
you need a whole book.

The Kind of Love I Imagine

the bottom two pairs of ribs in our bodies
do not make a full circle to the front.
when you put your arms
around my waist,
you complete
the circle.

-you are my protection.

he broke a
manic heart.
you have the chance
to love a
human
one.

-two very different relationships.

i long for an artist to be my lover.
i fantasize about our artwork framed
side by side on our living room walls,
capable of standing alone
but much more luxurious
when complimenting the other.

i yearn for cold winter nights
spent harmonizing
in front of the fireplace,
both with guitar in hand.

i imagine crisp fall mornings
spent photographing canada's north;
the vibrant colors captured beautifully by our lenses.
above all, i foresee our written works
featured one beside the other
at the local bookstore,
poetry inspired by the other's genuine love.
-oh, what a love that would be.

my eyes are the color of the oceans and skies.
his brown, the color of the earth.
together they complete the horizon:
sea-earth-sky.
-next we will take on the galaxy.

i was a camera
with faulty settings,
at times i overexposed,
i left things looking bright and whimsical.
halos flooded my image.
other times i underexposed.
i gave off a dull, flat feel.
darkness dominated my images.
you came along.
you said the images spoke to you.
i was not surprised.
your settings were not ideal either.
-imperfect.

your always
open arms
surround my body
like the tiny salt particles
that make up the dead sea.
they keep me afloat
when i think i might
be sinking.
-my support system.

admire their intricate exterior.
a closer look will reveal jagged lines
interspersed throughout their irises.
shades of blue and green
dominating their vibrant color palette.

alongside the lines,
you will see blotches resembling beads,
where their creator added some stand-out elements.

extending from their two corners,
black markings form the outline of a feather.
this is where the mascara has bled
from all the tears they have shed.

their pupils are the entrance points to my soul.
they determine whether the presence before them
will bring positive energy into my life
and they dilate or constrict accordingly.

my eyes are the most elaborate dream catchers.
they have a difficult decision at hand:
-should they allow you in?

you and i
are like two tectonic plates
converging into one another.
our mouths oozing with blistering lava
and our bodies afflicted with dangerous quakes
at every point of contact.
-do not get me wrong, i still want some chaos.

when i am with you
my chakras are at their most aligned.
my aura radiates the brightest shade of red
and reconstrues its boundaries to
welcome you into its reigns.
my ying and my yang perform a tribal dance
to the rhythm of your heartbeat.
my soul heals from its deeply embedded wounds.
you are better than any yoga practice
i have ever took part in.

-serenity.

on our first date,
it snowed mistletoes
from the sky.
-i told him he owed me a lifetime's worth of kisses.

hold her delicately.
rewind to the very beginning
and watch her story.
look for her plotline:
her ascent and her descent.
look for the characters in her life,
the ones that hurt her
and the ones that
brought her back to life.
do not fast forward.
experience things exactly the way
she experienced them.
moment by moment

when you reach the end,
do not be tempted to watch again.
you already know enough
to appreciate her wholly.
rest easy that there will be a part 2.
she has asked you to be a part of it.
-to be continued...

when i listen to you speak,
i do not hear the hoarseness
that makes up your country roots.
i hear the voice that will
sing our future little one lullabies.
there is a softness
about you.
-do not hide behind that tough exterior.

when i think of you,
i think of the letters XYQZ.
they do not spell love or lust
or anything lovey-dovey of that kind.
in the game of scrabble
these letters are the hardest to come by,
yet they generate the highest score.
i think of how long i waited
to meet someone like you
and how much i was rewarded
when I finally did.

-patience.

you defy the rule of thirds
i can position you anywhere in the frame:
middle,
top left,
bottom right,
the effect is the same.
my eyes are always drawn to you.

-you are art.

he held on tightly to the insides of her hands
and kissed her in the most surreal way
one would think possible.
as he pulled away,
she looked down at her palms
and saw a magnificent sight.

the crevice extending from her
little finger to her forefinger,
once faint and broken,
had grown into a
long, bold, consistent line.

it was magical.
he had reshaped her heart line,
after she thought she would be eternally tortured
with toxic love.
-palm reading.

instead of looking
for your reflection on a screen,
look deep into
a lover's
eyes.
i promise you
it will be the best selfie
you have ever seen.
-we need to start paying more attention to one another.

hand me your hand.
i will hand you mine.
we will intersect
our thumbs together
and shimmer our fingers,
creating a butterfly
with our own two hands.
-handshake for the soul.

i am a hummingbird
and you are the sweetest form
of red elixir
i flew backwards
forwards and
upside down
after i tasted
you
-you have quite the effect on me.

we have not met
in person just yet,
but i feel you are the type of guy
that would stand in front of me on our first date
and unroll a red carpet
as i walked

-high expectations.

he may not hold the
winning numbers,
but he is a lottery ticket,
a shot at love
just when my heart started to think
it would never again gamble.
-give everyone a chance.

like a bubble bath before bed,
hearing your voice once more
before the moon steals the day away
warms up my insides,
sets my skin aglow
and soothes my forever
overthinking soul.

-relaxation therapy.

he never once
called me
crazy
and that
meant the world
-acceptance

Regaining Identity

i am a weeping willow:
the tears that escape my core
trickle down my branches,
forming a puddle at my roots.
my only option is to absorb the water
and strengthen my roots, my core, my branches

-every bad experience makes you stronger.

i am partial:
i have no job.
i have no education.
i have no boyfriend.
i am sick.

i am also whole:
i have life experience.
i am knowledgeable.
i am loved.
i am eccentric.
-moving past the label.

ground yourself.
it will make
the falling more graceful
and the rising less intense.
-become one with your body.

they made her out to be a
delicate cherry blossom tree.
little did they know she had a history of
resilient giant sequoias in her bloodline.

-roots.

i do not fear heights, i told him.
i fear falling.
think of it more as flying not falling, he said,
then you'll be in the position of conqueror
rather than conquered.
-learn to use your wings.

a seasoned flyer
will be able to
guide a kite
through violent winds,
but the kite in itself must be
mighty.
-ask for help, but always find strength in yourself too.

aim to inspire.
leave a little imprint of yourself
in everyone that you meet
along your journey
of life.
essentially,
aim to be more than a star.
form networks.
aim to be part of a constellation.
-we are bigger than ourselves.

i peered through the window
and watched the thick snow fall to the ground.
there was a magical feel in the air.
it would be a white christmas!
i placed the last remaining ornament on the tree
and breathed a sigh of relief.
more importantly,
i would be home for christmas.
-just holding on until christmas.

since that day,
almost seven years ago now,
time is no longer measured in
years,
months,
days,
or hours.
time has taken on a new essence.
it is now time between relapses
or time passed from my last hospitalization
or time until the meds start working
or time until the side effects wear off
or looking for the smallest time difference for travel
to not disturb my circadian rhythm

i must breathe
and hope that soon
time will become living again
time will be warm cuban vacations
or a celebration of a birthday or anniversary
time will be that one concert
that everyone looks forward to going to in july
time will be milestones whether big or small
-time should not feel this heavy.

Seven Years Later

fighting a mental illness
is very much like being a professional fighter.
each episode represents one fight in the ring.
the end of an episode is the equivalent of a knockout.
you have battled your way through.
congratulations!

however, as in a physical fight, you will come out with bruises:
bruised friendships,
a bruised education,
a bruised identity.
some will fade away and eventually heal,
others will become more permanent.

your periods of remission are reminiscent of your training days.
you study tactics and strategies to better prepare yourself for the upcoming matches (episodes).
in the case of fighting,
perhaps you may be analyzing your previous fights
or working with a coach to improve your technique.
in regard to your illness,
this may involve identifying your warning signs
and working with a psychiatrist to better understand your illness.

unfortunately, you will not become a reputable fighter by winning
just one fight.
you must win one after the other,
regardless of the difficultly your opponent presents.
it is the same way with mental illness.
you must remember that just because you've won one fight,
does not mean there will not be more,
perhaps even harder than the first.
you must persevere,
and maintain a fighter's spirit throughout.

at first, i told people that i quit fighting,
that my fighting career was over.
i realized, however, that this was not true.
i was still fighting.
i had merely switched opponents
instead of a person,
i was fighting an illness.

i was definitely not a natural when it came to fighting
this new opponent.
things were shaky at first.
but with practice, i got better.
-i never really put down those gloves.

thank you:

people come from quite the distance
to see the most expansive waterfalls.
i was both humbled and grateful
that when ribbons of water began escaping my eyes,
i had family, friends, doctors and nurses
from near and far
by my side.

cupid sharpened his arrows,
he came looking for me.
i sharpened my pencils;
ready to rewrite anymore cursed love stories
he had waiting for me.

-my pen and pencils are my weapons.

when he says he needs space,
question him:
is it the type of space
where two are separated by a bridge,
free to join one another when they
see fit?
or is it such a space,
where an earthquake forms between you—
first as a little crack,
and then violently distancing you,
to a point of no return.
-the difference.

my dad always said not to go fishing,
after heavy rainfall;
the water gets murky,
and the fish cannot see the bait.
perhaps you have to clear up your own environment:
work on your dreams, goals, and aspirations.
set yourself up for the perfect catch.

-take care of yourself and the other half will come.

do the grass blades not dance beautifully in the wind?
-so why do we fear a sudden wind gust in our own lives?

i resorted to the garden,
a little mystified by my own state of mind
and experienced an illumination.
there was an owl hooting
in the distance; its undertone solemn,
empty, but very much persisting.
to compliment this hooting,
there were beautiful melodies of chickadees,
blue jays, and cardinals,
performing high-pitched bursts of crescendos
and diminuendos.
nature made sense of this mood state
that i longed so hard to articulate to friends:
how dark and bright could coincide in one.

-mixed state.

the sun's rays are projectors,
my eyes the screen
showing him all the darkness
my lifetime has seen.
-get to know me by a sunset.

with you there will be no need
to drive down memory
lane to remember
the good old days.
-all the days I have with you will continue to amaze.

you are the one
card in my hand that stayed tucked in
behind the rest.
-i thought i was going to fold, until i unveiled you.

for every verse i write,
i try to destruct
the label that has
been weighing on
me so heavily these last several
years.

-constantly defending my identity.

it is not necessary to have been in a
relationship to understand heartbreak.
it is enough to have mourned a spark
that once was.

-a lot of loves go unlived.

i know you wrote verses, too,
but you guarded them
from my prying eyes.
it is a shame i never
got to read the words
of the mind i fell in
love with.
-i remember the little things.

you were lightning strike
piercing my heart.
i counted my mississippis,
until you were out of town
but I could still hear you,
feel you, sometimes from far away.
every time i look into the mirror,
i still see that storm reflected in my
eyes.

-one mississippi, two mississipi, three mississipi…

i wish you would see how unevenly
the sun's rays hit my curls when
i water the daisies
every morning.
maybe you would judge me a little less harshly, then.
you would see that I am human.
-humans make mistakes.

if i had known that late august walk
would be the last time we would talk,
i would have you go from mister handshake
to mister hug in no time.

-why was our goodbye a handshake?

i looked up
and saw that the sky had turned
the color of cherry red lipstick
and magnotta red wine.
it is on days like this
when hell tempts heaven
that the perfect love stories align.
-genesis 3.

are you my mirror image,
my parallel line?
is that why my hips
and your arms never align?
-physics was never my strong point.

in your presence
i felt like an echo of myself.
you only need so many echoes
to trigger an avalanche.
-why we cannot stay friends.

an infatuation of such gravity
i wish to never see again.
this I am certain of.
feelings propelled by an overactive amygdala
and combusting synapses
that should have never been acknowledged
as love.
i can only hope i encounter
something more gentle,
something more genuine,
sustaining.
something real.

-does real love even exist for someone like me?

i stay concealed most of the time
these days,
not by choice,
but by necessity.

but when I do emerge,
i make quite the presence.

sometimes i surface
slowly, like the humpback
whale emerging for air.

other times i dazzle,
performing beautiful semi arcs,
in a dolphin-like fashion

and sometimes I appear stealthily
warning others only by a triangular fin.
but please when you do get a glimpse of me,
do say hello.
-i promise i do not bite.

if you doubt my intelligence
keep in mind
i may be blind to the obvious
but my eyes see the abstract.
-i see life through a kaleidoscope.

you will never have kids.
you can barely take care of yourself.

-(a parent's perspective); excuse me, but that is not your decision to make.

i did everything.
you know what the experts tell you to do:
i wrote the poems,
made the scrapbooks,
i even screamed at the top of my lungs
in the middle of the forest.
nothing helped.
i think it is one another's embrace
that can heal us now.
let them say we are pathetic.
let them laugh,
but they will never know our magic
and with it, they will never know our pain.

-i dreamt of you the other night, and for the first time in four years i did not have to apologize for it.

i was born into the 13th zodiac sign,
and he lives on cloud nine.
-do we exist?

i am a world champion
i am told.
i am a fighter.
i look like a star.
i am happy.
but do not even the strongest leaders deserve
a hand to hold,
words of console,
a chance to talk through emotions,
when they build up?
-i am a fighter, but I am no machine.

life may have you feeling stuck in a valley,
but what if it is protecting
you from the high winds above?
-earth, water, air, and fire.

i want to preserve
my friend's smiles in the form
of daisies which i will press flat
into my favorite poetry book
and look to for the days i cannot
see them.
-embedded forever.

first they silenced me
and now that i refuse to speak
they start an uproar.
-in their eyes i will always be the problem.

she did not realize how broken
she was
until something so harmonious,
so perfect,
so well intentioned
came her way
and all she could feel was fear
that it was not real,
that it would be taken away,
that she did not
deserve it.

-un(worthy)

like blood spewing from my aorta,
the words splattered out
on the page.
relentlessly
they helped me through the fog;
they helped me get through.

-toxic happiness; writing helped me cope and express what I was going through.

angel.

you were a different breed.
a superhero,
one of a kind.
your aura,
a real-life aura borealis,
glowing
first on earth and now in heaven.
this world was becoming too polluted
for your pure essence to exist.
God needed someone to help directing orders
up there.

you deserve the poetic expertise
of rupi kaur.
i am new to this craft.
but all I want for you is peace and warmth.
-nothing less than the cuban sun and God's tenderness in heaven.

Acknowledgments

First and foremost, I want to thank my family for being my support system during the most challenging times, especially my brother Gabriel for always making me laugh.

A huge thank you to my best friends for always being there for me when I needed a shoulder to cry on and for taking me on hikes when I needed an adventure or simply to get me out of the house. Natalie, you always said when I turn 25, that would be my year of change – well look at me now writing an acknowledgment with you in it.

Thank you to my doctor, nurse and healthcare providers for always supporting me on my journey to wellness. it is because of you that I feel comfortable seeking treatment and can truly accept the disorder I have.

Thank you to my publisher Carol Starr Taylor at Star House Publishing for reading my poems and seeing the potential for it in becoming a published book. Because of your faith in my work, the world can have a better understanding of what bipolar disorder entails.

Last but not least, thanks to Eminen – your music was my lullaby during mania.

About the Author

Viktoria D. Bednarczyk is an old soul trapped in a young body in Toronto, Ontario. Fun fact: owns a collection of over 15 diaries used completely. Another fun fact: 6 foot 2, with heels, probably 6 foot 5. Morning routine: waking up too early, refuses to drink coffee, and goes for a jog. Afternoon: explores her city throughout the day, striking up conversations with strangers. Evening routine: goes on a walk with friends, brainstorms lyrics/poems, takes a bath with Epson salts. Mode of transportation: the public bus. Mode of life: yoga and crystals. Favorite music genre: Country. Favorite food: pizza, but no pineapples. Favorite drink: Coke, not Diet Coke. definitely not Coke Zero. Favorite pastimes: dance and scrapbooking.

Her life is pretty simplistic, but she is more than okay with that.

www.ingramcontent.com/pod-product-compliance
Lightning Source LLC
Chambersburg PA
CBHW030925060726
47591CB00005B/1666

* 9 7 8 1 9 8 9 5 3 5 2 6 4 *